Vesak

Buddha's Birthday

It is Buddha's Birthday.
Some people
call this Vesak.

3

Vesak is a time to think about Buddha.

This is a **temple**.

We are praying

at the temple.

We will wash Baby Buddha.
We will put flowers
on Baby Buddha.

This is a **lotus flower**.

Lotus flowers are
very special.

Lotus flowers helped
Baby Buddha walk.

We will give gifts to the **monks**.
Some people will give food.
Some people will give flowers.

13

Vesak is special for us.

Glossary

 lotus flower

 monks

 temple